How to Hygge the British Way

About the Author

Jo Kneale has been a teacher, a mother, a teacher again, a teaching assistant and now an Office Ninja for her husband's law firm, Peter Kneale Solicitor. She's been good at hygge since she can remember, but only had a word for it in the last five years, when an unhealthy obsession with The Killing led to a fascination with all things Danish and a love of the concept of hygge.

Married for nearly 24 years to Peter, she has three teenage children and five guinea pigs at the moment. She likes to read, watch Game of Thrones and West Wing, visit cities with her husband and take part in TV quiz shows. Three to date, including The Chase where she won an amazing £47,000 by herself but had to share with the rest of the team, bringing home £20,000. That was a good day.

She's always wanted to write a book, and writing about hygge is what she does almost daily on her blog, How to Hygge the British Way. Jo believes that everybody can enjoy more hygge in their lives, they just have to recognise it.

Dedication:

This book is dedicated to my
Husband, Peter, without whose
patience and support it wouldn't
have been possible.
And to David, James and Sarah who
taught me to hygge when they were
children. Thank you for being such
good teachers.

Introduction to Hygge: What is it?

Oh, My Word!!! How BIG has hygge become? In 2015 you could mention hygge (as I did a lot) and everybody in the room would look at you weird, like you were swallowing a mouthful of poison or something. There were a couple of books that mentioned hygge in them, but usually in the context of 'this weird word that Danes use a lot' and never with the idea that this might be something that you... and yes, I mean you... could actually be good at.

That changed for a lot of people in September 2016, when Meik Wiking put his book, The Little Book of Hygge[1] out there and suddenly hygge was everywhere. From TV to radio, high-brow to low-brow, the word was on the lips of anyone who follows trends.

And often it was simply made out to be a trend. Like Hygge is so *now*... but next week it will be something else and all the hyggely items in the shop will be discounted. It was purveyed as a house style, a way of decorating that needed Scandinavian white walls and bare wooden floors, grey sofas and faux fur throws, hand thrown mugs and scented candles everywhere.

---

[1] Available on Amazon at https://www.amazon.co.uk/Little-Book-Hygge-Danish-Penguin/dp/0241283914/ref=sr_1_1?ie=UTF8&qid=1488198126&sr=8-1&keywords=the+little+book+of+hygge

Well, I'm sorry, but if you think hygge is just a trend or a decorating style then you've missed the point. Hygge has lasted for well over 200 years as a word in Denmark and that's not because they've been doing Mid Century Scandi Chic for that long. It's been grabbed at and kept close precisely because it's not a word that can be tied to one age or style or way of living. It's not even a thing, it's a feeling.

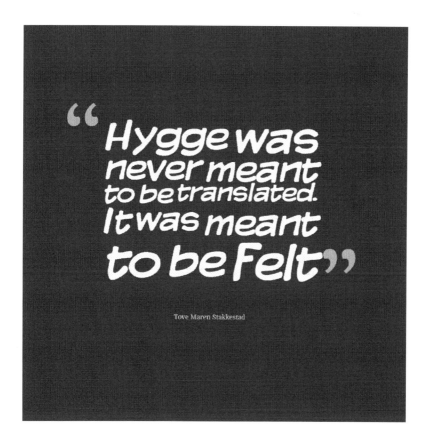

"Hygge was never meant to be translated. It was meant to be Felt"

Tove Maren Stakkestad

That's right. You can't point something out and say, "That thingumajig is hygge." Or even describe a thing as hyggely because the thing itself isn't the container of hygge. It might help you to feel hygge, or hyggely/hyggelig/hyggeligt but in and of itself it is just a thing. It's the interaction with and between the humans around the object that create the hygge. The thing might help you feel cosy/happy/secure/comfortable which creates the hygge in you, but that's different from claiming that any object in and of itself can make you feel hyggely/hyggelig/hyggeligt.

Hygge is the feeling you get when you come home after a long drive and you walk into the house. That "I'm back" sigh that you give when you've spent a tiring afternoon on an obligation visit with an old and cranky relative. It's the feeling you get when you slip your slippers on, curl up in your most comfortable chair and sip the first tea of a cold and wet winter's evening after a day at work. The bubble of contentment you have looking around in the pub when everybody is there and laughing at a silly joke and you feel that these are your people, this is your tribe.

It can be the feeling of presence that you get sitting next to a sleeping baby and smiling as they stick a leg in the air and keep sleeping. The security of a dog's head on your lap, the magic of watching the sun set through a tent flap as you & your friends laugh off the morning's rain. It is a mixture of feeling safe, happy, secure, surrounded by friends who've got your back, feeling content with life just as is, cosiness in the moment, an awareness of calm, an appreciation of fortune. It's not a feeling that will last forever, but it is a feeling that can last a while. Getting that explanation out in English takes a long time. In Danish, you just say you're feeling hyggely, or enjoying the hygge.

Let's sort out my language:

I know that hygge is a Danish/Norwegian word, and that in Denmark or Norway the adjectival form would be hyggelig or hyggeligt depending on gender. Right here and now I am telling you that I am British and I have nicked hygge forever to be a word in the English language so I am not going to keep being all *Danish Grammar Police* about hygge.

Therefore, my adjectival form is hyggely. To be full of hygge is to be hyggeful, and the past tense is I hyggered.

Clear? Good. Now, where was I?

" Remember that lovely evening, surrounded by friends at home, maybe with a glass of wine or cup of tea and baked goods on the table. There were candles, the rain was beating on the window outside. There was laughter, conversation and a feeling of comfort.... you were present in the moment together. There was no before or after that mattered. That was hygge. "

Bronte Aurell

Hygge is meant to be different for everyone, but will probably have some shared attributes.

1. Mostly hygge happens in small groups. A big party won't be hyggely, a group of 4 to 6 eating and hanging out together will be.

2. You can hygge alone, but like sex it's better with a friend. There's something about sharing a special moment that magnifies the feeling.

3. You won't be feeling hyggely all day every day. And anybody who says otherwise hasn't got the right idea. Hygge is a pause in real life, not the whole life. You will still have the washing to do, the bills to pay and the house to clean, but after (or in the middle) of all that, you will have time to carve out a breather and a moment to rest.

4. Food plays a big part but guilt doesn't. Whatever food is your hygge treat, you won't eat it and feel guilty. This does tie into number 3, though, because you won't be eating your hygge treats all the time either. They're treats for a reason, right? Most of the time your diet will be healthy, nutritious and full of benefits. Your hygge treats can be healthy, too, if that's what you like, otherwise they'll be treats that you enjoy. And you will eat them mindfully, with relish, and with enjoyment. No guilt.

5. Hygge can take place inside or outside the house. It's not dependent on location, just emotion. Take a friend to the beach at sunset (I live on the West coast of England) and enjoy a hyggely moment watching the sun set over the water. No cushions, no candles, just hygge. Similarly, an afternoon crashed on the grass at

the park can be hygge if it's a chance to breathe, catch up with friends, share food, fun and happiness.

Hopefully this book will give you 50 ways to bring more hygge into your home. None of them are expensive (I won't be telling you to go to Denmark to study hygge in its home country) and most are actually free. Some are actions, others are things for you to think about. You don't have to do them all, or any, as long as you know what hygge as you consider it to be needs to exist.

Okay, how is this book arranged? Well, there are 5 chapters arranged around themes: Hygge in the home, in the workplace, how to hygge with a family, hyggering for your soul and a fifth chapter of hygge resources. Each one is a list of ways to introduce or expand on hygge in that area. Some ideas will be so familiar to you, you'll be looking up to heaven and asking "What's new in that?" Others will be ideas you may not have thought of as hygge, but they are. Everything should be easy enough to do, not cost a fortune, and should help to create a feeling of hygge. There are no guarantees, so if you have the hyggiest house and still aren't feeling it, perhaps you need to approach it differently. Hygge isn't competitive. It can't be caught and it won't be bought.

1: Hygge Your Home

The home is the usual base for hygge. It's the place where you spend most of your relaxation hours, the place where you sleep, often the place where you work nowadays. It's worth getting it to be a hyggely spot, so that you can relax and enjoy time there, with or without other people. Does this take a fortune? **No**. In fact, hyggering up your home can be done very cheaply and easily if you understand what hygge truly is.

1. **Don't sweat the small stuff.** Your home is your home and the only person it needs to suit is you.

   On my hygge journey I soon came to realise that a lot of the articles I was reading were actually just trying to sell me something: a throw, a seat, a cushion, a jumper, candles, candles or more candles. They also all had the same aesthetic: a cool, Scandinavian mid-century chic with white walls and grey throws. Hell for people who hate cleaning and can get a white top dirty within 5 minutes. And everything in the articles had a label....

   I don't know about you, but I haven't got a bottomless pit of money to spend on making a house into a hygge home, but I do love my home and family.

A huggelig home is a home that feels lived in; a home that reflects who you are and tells your story.

Trine Hahnemann

howtohyggethebritishway.com

If the hygge candle and the false fur throw suit your style, then go for it. If not, then recognise what is your style and try to make sure that whatever comes into your house suits you. Having hand thrown mugs to drink from won't make the tea made just for you with love by your daughter taste any better.

Having said that, reading the articles on conspicuous hygge consumption can be very good for your mental health. My favourite one is this one. http://www.luxurylondon.co.uk/article/how-to-hygge-your-home Just sit down to read it, and don't read it anywhere where you can't laugh out loud.

2. **You'll never have a perfect home.**

   Give up on the image now. We are so used to seeing representations of perfection all over the place now, we forget that real life is actually quite messy. This is the downside of Pinterest and Social Media. We can see perfect homes every minute of every day, but they're not totally achievable. Nobody lives like that all the time, or the effort to keep up a home like that would take up so much mental and physical power that there wouldn't be time for anything else. And I like the everything else of life. I am happy to let my home be the physical embodiment of my brain: a little of everything all mixed together. I'm not a perfectionist, and that suits me fine.

3. **You have everything you need to hygge at home.**

   Just look around and find it. I'm betting that your home is probably already quite hyggely for you, simply because it is your home and you will have chosen the things in it.

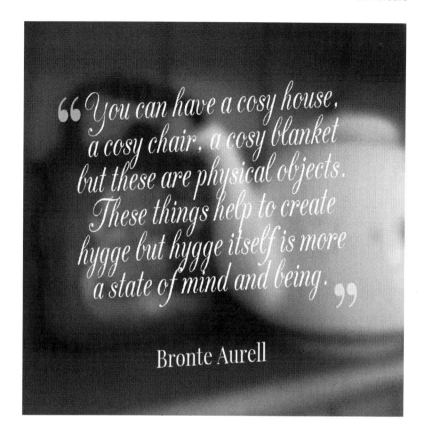

"You can have a cosy house, a cosy chair, a cosy blanket but these are physical objects. These things help to create hygge but hygge itself is more a state of mind and being."

Bronte Aurell

Hygge is more about the people and the atmosphere than the contents of a room, but having comfortable stuff helps to create a comfortable feeling. A few cushions, blankets, a pile of magazines or books that you enjoy, having flowers in season or just a few pinecones or conkers scattered on the entrance table can all help you relax and feel cosy/comfy/secure. Here's a list of things that members of The Hygge Nook on Facebook swear by for encouraging (not creating) hygge:

17

- A Real Fire. I don't have a real fire that works, but I have to admit the pictures of wood-burning stoves I've seen do look very appealing. My second brother does have one, so family parties on cold days are very hygge most of the time. Some members of The Hygge Nook cheat and use a Fireplace programme on their TV to give the look, with none of the cleaning or heat.

- A Comfortable Seat. This could be a settee or an armchair. So long as it is a comfortable shape and size for you, that will do.

- Fairy lights. Not just at Christmas. The Hygge Nook-worms (members of The Hygge Nook) use them on mantelpieces, in jars, strung over branches. I had a string in my unused fireplace that was lovely to light at night... until the guinea pigs chewed the wires. Now my fairy lights lie along my mantelpiece and look beautiful shining through the tealight holders even on days when I don't light the candles.

- Soft lighting. I'm not a lighting tyrant. I know different people will love or hate candles. I know people are allergic to them or have chest complaints, so I'm not going to tell you to get a whole host of candles and light them every day. I will say that there are few light sources as

18

beautiful on a cold, dark night, and that tealights don't cost the earth to buy. Candle or not as you like, try to have adaptable lighting in your home. My husband would have the main light on all night long while he reads and watches TV. I love turning the lamps on around the room and having gentle pools of lighting that soften the place and hide the dust. And don't forget, if you can't have candles because of allergies, children, pets or a fear of soot, there are some really good false alternatives out there. If you can't have the real thing, fake it.

- Bringing nature inside. This could be as simple as a bunch of flowers, as cheap as a pile of conkers collected on an Autumn afternoon's walk or as basic as a rock on the desk. Whichever and whatever, it's a natural object to touch, admire and remind you that the planet has been here long before you and will be here a long time after…. Enjoy the moment.

4. **Hygge doesn't mean you have to change your style.** If you love Scandinavian white chic, go for it. Into tribal prints? They're hygge too. Or cottage style, or chic monochrome. As long as it suits you and you feel cosy there, then it's hyggelig. My own home is probably a wild mix of cottage twee with Boho Eclectic. It's got no

19

particular style, plenty of colour and everything is second hand or charity shopped. (or Ikea... I like Ikea's bookshelves). There is no way my home will ever be bare floors and white walls, so if hygge relied on them I'd be done for. Fortunately, hygge the way I practise it will never be dependent on furnishings. I pile my cushions high with pride, my husband throws them to the floor with disgust. We agree to disagree.

5. **Keep your house clean rather than tidy**.

   A beautiful smell and a warm smile will overcome a few piles on the floor most of the time. Also, if you're British then clean trumps tidy any day. I try to concentrate on keeping my most public rooms fit for human habitations and having the rest clean enough. I am not the most house-proud homemaker. I'd rather have the cake in the oven and the smiles on the kids' faces than be nagging about the mess. They will only be this age once... and only living at home for a finite amount of time... so I make the most of them while I can. I also use them for housework as well.

6. **Create a hygge nook**.

   A hyggekrog (the proper Danish word) is a place in the home where you can comfortably do things that often lead to a feeling of hygge. Creating corners cosy enough to encourage you to stay and rest means that the space to feel hyggely is available. I like to c[...] places my hygge nook. Do you have a seat you[...] most comfortable in? A corner of a room that's your[...] favourite for reading or watching TV? Then you've got the start of a hygge nook.

Add a lamp to read or craft by, use a table to showcase books that are meaningful or particularly lovely to touch or smell. You may want to display something from your past, or a photograph that has particular meaning for you. This is your hygge nook and you can fill it with things that make you feel hyggely.

7. **You can create Hygge Nooks outside of the home.**
You possibly have a favourite place in a coffee shop… I love sitting in the corner of our Friday coffee shop, facing the door. My husband laughs and says I always pick the Mafia seat, because nobody can creep up on me there, but I say I sit there because it gives me a good view of all the people and I love to watch people! And yes, we have a Friday coffee shop and a Sunday coffee shop. I am actually in the process of setting up a Saturday coffee shop with a friend as well! We go every week at about the same time, and the regular staff smile when they see us.

8. **If you don't have it, make it.**
Or borrow it, or save up for a special thing.

memade, and very often the act of creating nore hygge time and feelings. The time and it you put into making a blanket or cushion, be paid back by the positive feeling of pride nade it yourself.

When I first started blogging I read a lot of crochet blogs, because I couldn't crochet, only knit and I always felt like I was missing out on something. Finally, spurred on by Attic 24[2], I bought wool to make a blanket, used YouTube as my teacher and got crocheting. Now I have throws in every shade in every room, and I'm moving on to crocheting with colour and using different stitches. I'm still learning, but the pride I feel in my first straggly efforts is still immense.

There are lots of things that can boost the hygge in your home that you can make. How about tealight jars? A simple lace or ribbon trim around a jam jar elevates it into an object worthy of being on the mantelpiece. Sewing, crochet, knitting, paper-crafting, painting, pyrography, there are a host of activities out there suitable for making things for your home. Pick one that you fancy and try it out.

---

[2] Attic 24 is a wonderful lifestyle website... well, actually it's more like the story of a family who live in Skipton, Yorkshire and the Mum's skill in crochet. It's colourful, bright, mostly optimistic and like a ray of golden sunshine on a grey day. Go find her at http://www.attic24.typepad.com/

Hygge is
the basic
language
of comfort.

LouisaThomsenBrits

www.howtohyggethebritishway.com

Worst case scenario, you make nothing fit for human vision and keep it in a drawer (or chuck it out). Best case scenario, your makes decorate the house and visitors ask, "Oh my, where does that darling thing come from?"

In wisdom from another age, Wordsworth said, "The world is too much with us; late and soon, Getting and spending, we lay waste our powers:" and I think we do seem sometimes to be on a treadwheel of earning and spending on things that ultimately won't matter.

9. **Simplify, Simplify, Simplify**.

Thoreau this time. "Our life is frittered away by detail... simplify, simplify, simplify."

And it is true that the more complicated our lives become, the more time it takes us to do anything. Having every corner full of stuff makes a quick clean up impossible. Covering every surface with items, no matter how lovely, takes up visual space and makes our actions harder. Visual clutter impacts our ability to process information quickly[3], and thus impacts upon our time available. Look around your house with a critical eye. Do you have things out on display that make you frown? Does everything in your house suit you? Are there items you have because they were given or donated as gifts and not to keep them out would be rude, even though Aunt Marge never visits or (in some cases) died 10 years ago?

Don't be afraid to box up or clear out and start over with a blank space to put back in the things that say home to you now. Many people swear by the Konmari method[4], and I do fold my clothes now before putting them vertically in my drawers so I can see what I have. Google Konmari clothes folding and see what I mean.

---

3   https://unclutterer.com/2011/03/29/scientists-find-physical-clutter-negatively-affects-your-ability-to-focus-process-information/

4 Marie Kondo wrote a seminal book on tidying up, "The Life Changing Magic of Tidying Up." It is really good, or visit her website https://konmari.com/

One day, I promise myself... one day I'll (
house.

Making sure that our houses are running as
possible can take some of the burden of choic ..vay.
There are loads of great sites out there with advice on
simplifying the life we lead. Try simplifying your
wardrobe, using 33/3 project[5], or clearing the house
using the Konmari method. Housecleaning in 20
minutes a day was the subject of an article on
Apartment Therapy in 2010[6]

How does this connect to hygge, you ask? Well, being
able to sit with friends and not feel that the house is a
mess, or that you need to be doing something else
means that you can relax as a host or a guest... and a
relaxed atmosphere is the best place to feel hygge.
Also, guests relax better if they don't have to worry
about knocking a pile of books over, or that the table
they need to put their tea on will have an avalanche.

10. **Curate your world carefully.**

---

[5] http://bemorewithless.com/project-333/ Courtney Carver set out to use just 33
items of clothing over 3 months. It's extreme, but it does work for keeping your
choices limited. I'm not that brave. I'd rather go down the Steve Jobs route and
have 100 black tops and 10 pairs of black trousers in the same style. Jazz it up with
scarves and jewellery, and it can look different every day. Oh, who am I kidding? I
have a colourful wardrobe full of clothes that I love and wear on rotation.

[6] http://www.apartmenttherapy.com/how-to-clean-your-house-in-20-minutes-a-day-
for-30-days-131142

This connects on to the act of simplification in number 9. Once you have your world sorted out so that its care is as simple as possible, wouldn't it be silly to then open the floodgates and let anything back in? Again, I turn to Marie Kondo as the expert: If a thing doesn't spark joy... proper joy, not just a slightly happy feeling... then you can probably do without it for a while. You can do this throughout your home and life, but remember to apply it to any shopping you do as well. Everything you bring into your home and life should be something you have thought about and decided positively that you need.

In hygge terms, you need to make the space to enjoy yourself and other's company. If you are forever chopping and changing to suit fashion or trends, then you will never reach the point of comfort. Sure, your mind will be dancing to the power of novelty and purchase (for an interesting article on the neuroscience behind shopping, see this article http://mag.ispo.com/2015/01/90-percent-of-all-purchasing-decisions-are-made-subconsciously/?lang=en) but hygge needs us to look beyond, to stop buying unconsciously on auto pilot and to learn again to appreciate what we have.

Never buy anything straight away, either write your shopping list beforehand, have a Wants list that you add the item to or give yourself 24 hours' grace, especially on big purchases, to think things over.

I love having the time to shop, see things and then walk away without buying. If I really want the thing, if it stays with me and I can see myself, in my mind's eye, using it and needing it, then I'll go back and buy. If I walk away and the object has no real impression on me, then buying it would probably have been a waste of time, money and space. I had this happen to me recently when out shopping. I saw a backpack I love[7] in a variety of colours. I already have one of these backpacks, they're fashionable now and I wondered about getting a new, brighter colour for the spring. I couldn't imagine which one would suit me best, so I walked away thinking to myself that if I had a clear picture of me with a colour in my head the next day I'd go back and get that colour. I'm still wondering which colour I could get, but now (at least 7 days later) I know that I don't actually want the backpack, more the idea of the backpack or the novelty of the new thing. I may get one for my birthday, as a present off the husband, or I may not. I'm not desperate to get one at all. If I'd given in on that first day, I would have impulse purchased a back pack that I wouldn't need.

---

[7] http://www.fjallraven.co.uk/equipment/kanken?gclid=CjwKEAiAuc_FBRD7_JCM3N SY92wSJABbVoxBe8MPfau4EWfw22r5KNPOaflOLwBiLBFc8WvsHTLRqBoCluDw _wcB&model=952

11. **Make the Kitchen the Heart of the Home**.

I don't know about you, but the liveable kitchens in magazines with Agas, large tables, sofas stuffed in the corner, cabinets full of crockery used often and a welsh dresser taking pride of place make my heart sing. I have happy memories of time spent in the kitchens of Irish relatives, where the room really is lived in all the time, and of sharing hot whiskey toddies, passing around food, swapping jokes and sharing stories. Long evenings of hygge. Lovely.

I would love to have a multi-use kitchen, where the children play and do homework, with a table big enough to eat most meals at and where the family are automatically drawn to as the first place to stop off when they arrive. I don't have a kitchen like that at all, nowhere near. My kitchen is small, dark, slightly frayed at the edges and has no space for more than 2 people to work together. It's a sad lack in my life.

A fellow hygge Nookworm wrote this in answer to my question "Is the kitchen the Heart of the Home?"

"In our house it literally is where all life happens, meals cooked and eaten together, decisions made and conversations had round the kitchen table, birthdays, Christmases, high days and holidays celebrated, countless broken hearted tears wiped, advice asked for and given, minor surgery performed on friends who come to us after

accidents happen!, table tennis tournaments played, dancing and disco lights, workmen fed and watered, crafts done, objects fixed and painted.....it is the entrance to our home! I often come down and find someone has let themselves in and made themselves at home in the kitchen! No matter how many other rooms and comfy seats we have, the kitchen table is where everyone gravitates to and stays 9 times out of 10. It truly is the beating heart of our home for everyone, and I wouldn't have it any other way."

I quite agree that, where practical, the kitchen makes a beautiful heart of the home; that as the source of warmth, food and fellowship it makes sense to make it the heart of hygge. If you can do that, if you can create the kitchen as the most-used room in your house, I say God Bless You and how lucky are you?! Being able to hygge in a warm area full of food is ideal.

But even if your kitchen is a broom cupboard, you can still have a heart of the home. You just have to think laterally. In our house the living room has taken over as the space where everyone meets first, where hygge is made most, where we share treats and drinks. It's probably the room that holds our 'spirits' most, in a jolly sense rather than anything hocus-pocus style.

When you walk in to the living room, you know there's a family, with pets, with a lot of different interests and a great deal of readers. It's furnished with hand-me-downs and well-loved pieces of furniture, all very comfortable, and it has lamps around the outside that cast pools of light and very often candles lit in the evening all through the year.

My Welsh Dresser in the Dining Room is red, because the original pine colour didn't suit the rest of the furniture.

I have plans eventually to move the kitchen and expand it into a living space, but until the money tree blooms those plans are on hold.

Do you have a heart of the home? If not, why not? What can you do about it? Think hard, and try out a few alternatives. You may find that with a little ingenuity you find a room that works as well as the kitchens of old. Or not. Ultimately, you'll find a workable solution, and stick to it in the end. It's worth making a room that feels so comfortable people just want to be there.

12. Luxury isn't hygge.

Hygge loves simplicity and a lack of excess. We had an interesting conversation on The Hygge Nook one day about an advert for Hygge and Champagne Dinner Party meals[8]; a chef would come to your home and cook the meals for you, which would be served with champagne and silver service (silver service is how they used to serve things at dinnertime in Downton Abbey: it basically means being waited on and not doing a thing to help yourself) The question was: was this hygge? The consensus was that, no, it was not. The whole getting an expert in to cook for a meal in the home seemed too much like conspicuous consumption to be hygge. And yet, these are being sold as hygge

---

[8]   http://www.independent.co.uk/life-style/food-and-drink/hygge-and-champagne-dinner-party-winter-cold-wine-a7423556.html

meals. We also had an interesting side discussion about when would it be hygge to drink champagne… this was actually ruled as possible in a hyggely situation if a. the champagne was a gift and b. you served it with ordinary food, rather than posh grub, to lessen the luxury of the item.

Hygge wasn't ever meant to mean luxury. In so many ways what it stands for… equality, togetherness, welcoming all levels together…. is so against luxury. Comfort, yes: luxury, no. Meik Wiking told me in an interview for my blog[9], "Hygge is about an atmosphere rather than things. Luxury is not hygge. Togetherness, gratitude, simplicity is."

What does that mean for a hygge fiend? Well, it means looking around your house with an eye focused on comfort ahead of brand awareness, of being clear that the place will look lived in, welcoming, a happy place to be, before thinking whether the rug, picture, glass vase or table come from the Right Shop. The hygge home will be just as lovingly furnished from a charity shop, with careful purchasing, as from a high-end retailer.

---

[9] https://howtohyggethebritishway.com/2016/10/15/the-hyggemaster-is-in-the-house-meik-wiking-answers-some-of-my-questions-about-hygge/ He's very keen to stress that there is no competition in hygge, that one person won't be better than another, just different.

Hygge happens when we commit to the pleasure of the present moment in its simplicity. It's there in the things we do that give everyday life value and meaning, that comfort us, make us feel at home, rooted and generous.
LouisaThomsenBrits

www.howtohyggethebritishway.com

And the nix to luxury extends to wardrobe and food as well. Buy good quality that lasts, not fashion that fades after a season. Timelessness never goes out of fashion. Food wise, eschew the most expensive brand names to try out own-label or unbranded stuff. In blind tastings the discount stores such as Lidl or Aldi often do well ahead of the more prestigious retailers[10]. Why pay more? To impress your friends? Because you can? Or because it just looks good? If you know that a luxury

10   http://www.huffingtonpost.co.uk/entry/best-champagne-for-christmas-2016-aldi_uk_582dad0ce4b0c6c8bc14d8ff

product is miles better and worth it, then I say go for it. But if you honestly know the only reason you buy luxury is to impress your guests... well, impress them a different way. Get real flowers for their bedroom, or take some time to put the finishing touches to the room, like scent or fresh fruit. The labels don't impress me anymore. This isn't the 1980's.

13. **Create a Focal Point.**

Time and again a fireplace or wood-burning stove show up in the pictures hashtagged #hygge on Twitter and Instagram. It's no wonder, the power of flames to draw the eye and keep people focused is so well known that the word *focus* actually comes from the Latin word for 'hearth'.

There's a magic in the flame that draws the eye, and fire holds a magical place yet in the hearts of men. Consider how often it's used as a metaphor for power, for love, for destructive force, for life itself. And how pleasant it is to waste an hour or two watching the flames, letting your thoughts drift like the smoke.

In my first married home, we didn't have a fireplace, just a gas fire that sat forlornly in the centre of the wall. It was a new house, which had superb insulation, and the fire was rarely if ever lit. My home now has a fireplace, with a living flame gas fire and, again, perfect insulation. The fire itself is never on. But the hearth is there and it gives the room a focus that I like to make the most of by using candles and decorating according to the seasons. With crafty use of fairy lights and candles, there can be a false-fire most evenings. I'm happy with that, but I still enjoy pinning a good few fireplaces and stoves on Pinterest.

My fire watching at home is a summer sport. In the garden, in my seating area, we have a fire-pit, made of metal and used a fair bit on balmy summer evenings to gather around. It comes in very useful indeed during exam season when a tired school child will often sit there and relax after revision, letting the stresses float away....

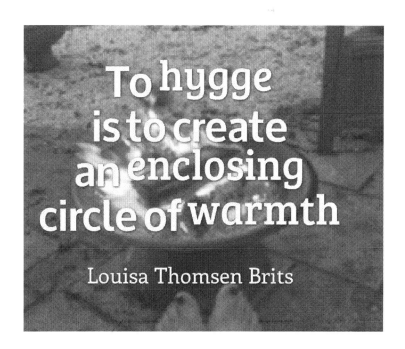

To hygge is to create an enclosing circle of warmth

Louisa Thomsen Brits

Fire-pits are available quite cheaply, and wood needn't cost a bomb. Remember to light the fire in a safe area, away from trees and bushes and never to leave the fire burning unattended. Also, take particular care with children and fire. But I'm teaching my grandmother how to suck eggs here, you're adult and sensible enough and you know that it's better your child learns the rules of fire watching sensibly as young as possible under your supervision.

Both inside and outside fire provides a focal point. If you haven't got either, do cheat. Masses of candles on a mirror tray or in front of a mirror can still generate a fair amount of light and the flickering flames are just as useful for drawing the eye.

14. **No home is complete without a book**:

I use them to decorate the house. Even in these modern days of Kindles and e-reading apps, there is something so enticing about an actual physical book. I don't know whether it's the feel, the smell or the anticipation, but books are holding their own in a world of electronic trickery[11]. Perhaps because they don't need charging??

All my houses have come with plenty of blank walls to put shelves against, and there are few things more

---

[11]   https://www.macobserver.com/analysis/surprise-hardback-book-sales-overtake-e-books-despite-ipad-iphone/

gratifying than using books to fill the shelves. By choosing your favourites, or finding your out-of-print heroes in a hardback version, you can decorate the house in a very hyggely way. Being surrounded by the heroes of your youth, or middle age, gives you a great feeling of comfort. And you are never alone with a book.

One is never ALONE with a BOOK nearby, don't you agree? Every page reminds us of a day that has passed and makes us RELIVE the emotions that filled it. Arturo Pérez-Reverte

www.howtohyggethebritishway.com

I have a small windowsill in my downstairs cloakroom toilet that holds a small selection of Persephone[12]

---

[12] Persephone books is a London publisher specialising in 20th Century women's writers that are out of print or forgotten. Their books are cool grey works of art. Find them at http://www.persephonebooks.co.uk/

books, their elegant grey covers set off the deep maroon and cream of the walls.

More books sit next to my bed, novels and self-help books. This is where the novels of my life live. The Jane Eyre dates from 1936 and was my grandmothers. I have a copy of The Harvester by Gene Stratton Porter passed to me by my mother and soon to be passed on to my daughter. Precious Bane, Princess Bride: I could tell you when each of these entered my life and how much I owe them for making me the person I am today. Each one here has been carefully selected, and that's my best advice to you. Choose well which books to keep. Choose them for their effect on you, and don't be put off by what anyone else thinks. Life is lived as an individual: don't lose that power.

And be prepared to talk about them as well. I find people will often scan along a bookshelf and look at things in a way they wouldn't do with your underwear drawer, and yet the books you read and choose to hold on to very often say more about you than the undies you wear.

15. **Take your hygge outside as well**.

Do you have a garden? Then for a large portion of the year, that should be one of your hygge-nooks. You only need a seat and a glass of something cooling to turn an ordinary summer's evening into a wondrous feeling. Scrub needing the seat; so long as the grass is dry enough, a blanket spread over it will do.

My garden suffers from the fact that I have black fingers. Plants, especially flowers, see me and die. But I have a lawn that is big enough to lie on and a corner sheltered from the wind where I can sit on cushioned chairs and share a hyggely time with friends or family. If the temperature drops, we light a fire, but in glorious summer days the seating area is under the shade of the trees and often the coolest part of the garden.

Making this into an outdoors room makes sense. When my children were young and summer holidays felt every minute of the six weeks long, we sat out most days long into the evening and played. We used bamboo poles and blankets to build forts, we played in the sprinkler to keep cool, we just sat and had stories together instead of watching endless TV. Lunch was a picnic, and often supper was eaten outside as well.

It's harder in the years when the heavens open and every day is a rainy day, but it's still worth getting outside the house. Rain never hurt anyone and you will find that the air during and after the rain seems different. Some claim there is more oxygen in it, others that the rise in negative ions makes you feel different. All I know is I love the smell and that there is officially a word for the smell of rain on dry ground: petrichor.

Size doesn't matter. Look up *small backyard* ideas on Pinterest and you'll see that a small space can be even more hyggely than a massive one. It's that intimacy thing again, where closeness adds to the bonding experience. Even a sunny front step is a good place to sit outside if it means you meet your neighbours and build a community. Take pride in your outside space, and add it to your cleaning routines if it needs it.

41

The home is such a centre of hygge, it's worth walking around and making sure that it feels right. Whether you own your own house or you're renting a small flat, for however long you are there this space is yours. Own it, love it, do what you can for it in terms of accessories, cleanliness, keeping it tidy. A home is a place of love and *love*… true love…. Is the basis of all hygge.

2: Hygge your workplace

In Britain we work for an average of 42.7 hou employment[13]. That's a lot of time at work. No wonder it feels sometimes like all we do is sleep and work. Putting aside the mental and physical toll it takes on us, working that hard is difficult, especially if you're in an office you don't feel comfortable in. What can we do about it, though? Well, applying some hygge principles to your work may not lessen the hours but it could help you to be happier in the time you spend there.

1. **Work smarter, not longer**. Use the best productivity techniques to mean that you get as much done in the official work times as others do burning the midnight oil. And have days when you are strict about the time you leave. Can you make sure that most Fridays you can leave on the dot? How about another day midweek when you claim back your time? Use an hour after work to foster better relations in the office, by going out for a drink or a coffee with a colleague. Or if your job really is crazily time-intensive, can you steal back time another way? The point is to give yourself a break, and a defined stop to work. Turn off the emails at lunchtime,

---

[13] https://www.theguardian.com/news/datablog/2011/dec/08/europe-working-hours

switch off the phone and just be for an hour. You can catch up with work after that. Even slaves had to rest.

Take your time back. You do not owe anything to anyone else once you leave your desk. Bronte Aurell

www.howtohyggethebritishway.com

I find Getting Things Done[14] by David Allen is one of my preferred planning methods. With its use of project pages, definable steps and organising thoughts according to where the action will be completed, you can use it to plan both home and office work. And an integral part of its running procedure is a review over the past work and towards the future tasks that makes you prioritise, but there are other productivity

[14] http://gettingthingsdone.com/

techniques that work as well. The Pomodoro Technique[15] is a time-management technique that helps people to use time well. It also works with a planning principle like Getting Things Done. I've just never found a timer pretty enough to encourage me to use it regularly, plus I'm a natural at taking breaks in the office.

Ask the workers you see getting their work done in an acceptable time frame what their secret is. It may be that a productivity idea they found or a book that they've read could help you carve some space into your life.

2. **Make one day a week Cake Day in the office.**

Take in a homemade cake or buy a cake to share. Either stop for a short while mid-morning or afternoon, or put it out to share at lunchtime. Make sure you invite the Boss, so that s/he sees the benefits of a happy workforce: who knows, it might encourage them to buy the cake some weeks! If you stick with it and it's a success, then ask around to share the cost, or start a collection to pay for it.

Food is always a great way to build community. At one place I worked, everybody shared a lunch on Friday. Some weeks it was sandwiches, other times they had takeaway or ordered in from a caterer. The cost was

---

[15] http://cirillocompany.de/pages/pomodoro-technique

45

shared and kept low enough so that everybody could join in. I only worked mornings at the time, but I always stayed later on a Friday lunchtime to enjoy the hygge. It was a lovely way of building a team of staff. They were cracking in other ways too, always looking out for each other and bringing in snacks and treats to share. It was really one of the nicest places I've ever worked, and I think that was partly because they had such a history of sharing food and partly because they never made me feel like a temporary member of staff.

Treats and hygge go together.

Bronte Aurell

www.howtohyggethebritishway.com

Cake sales are also great ways to raise money for charity: it also helps you to feel that the money invested in the cakes was actually money raised for the charity of your choice.

3. **Use a planner to take the burden of organising out of your head**.

It's a proven fact that the act of writing things down makes you more likely to do them[16]. I'm a bullet journal fan, so I write everything down in my notebook and then I check it off on completion. To find out more about bullet journaling go to Ryder Carroll's website http://bulletjournal.com/. Remember that I only use mine as a simple list, not a memory book and then go searching Pinterest for bullet journals. They can be as simple or as fancy as you like…. The notebook doesn't matter, but finding one that suits you and getting everyday use out of it is a wonderful feeling. Mine varies between an orange Leuchtturm 1917, which comes highly recommended by the Facebook groups that have inspired me, or a Filofax. Yes, I am a yuppie. I'm a very minimalist user, no fancy types or pictures, but if you do get sucked in to the world of Bujo-ing, then drawing up the pages and adding details like colours and stickers to them can be a very hyggely moment in the week.

---

[16] http://www.positivityblog.com/index.php/2010/09/30/write-things-down/ among others. Some of them are manifesting blogs, which I've kept away from here, but I do actually believe that if you write a goal down and believe in it, it's more achievable.

I also break my tasks down into the constituent parts, list them and then check them off. Not only do I do most of my planning and thinking about planning up front, the satisfaction of ticking off or marking the boxes is not to be undervalued. And I plan in my fun, so I know that I will enjoy the quiz tonight, or that I plan to go to the cinema on Tuesday.

Of course, you can use a digital calendar or planning app to do this just as well, but there is still something to be said for having the list in black and white in front of you and ready to tick off items as you go along. I'm a checklist fan, and I love seeing my list complete (No. Not often).

4. **Take a Good Look at the Office**.

   Can you hygge it up a bit?

   This, of course, depends on who you are and what your role in the office is. I'm the Office Manager for my husband's small solicitor's firm in Liverpool. I got to decide everything design-wise to do with the firm: the colours, the materials, the décor were all my choice. That's why the office is a calming shade of not orange and not brown. It's not terracotta either. The paint shade is called Nectarine Spice, but that means nothing really. I liked it because it wasn't too vibrant but had life. And it looks good with black and white.

48

Sadly, colour is an enemy to many offices, it seems. Because I work on reception, my desk has to be clear(ish) and ready to greet people. There's still room for a little hygge though, like my candle, my owl mascot and my pencil pot shaped like a hand… quirky, but fun. I'm also looking out for a picture for the wall, but it has to be the right picture. I'll know it when I see it.

If my desk weren't on public display, I'd hygge it up even more. I know people who work in cubicles who use fairy lights to make their area seem less official. Candles, plants, individual touches like photos or small figurines can all be used to make your office a home from home. At Christmas I really indulged in a table top tree and a wooden decoration. It gave me pleasure every time I looked at it.

Getting nature into the office is a health-full thing to do as well. Plants are always beneficial in an indoor environment, with spider plants and lemon balm both well known to improve the atmosphere there! And in a small office like ours, plant welfare is down to me as well, which means I have to remember to take care of them, giving me a chance in work to show my gentle, caring side.

5. **Rituals matter in the workplace as well**.

   In Part 3 I am going to write about the power of rituals and routines to ground the family and help them grow. Rituals matter in the office just as much. The habits we develop tell people much about us, and what are rituals except habits practised by a number of people at the same time? They should be done often enough to be familiar, relevant enough to make sense and easy enough to keep to.

Sometimes rituals are big, whole office things... think of the Christmas Night Out as one of these... and other times the ritual is a more intimate affair. My husband had to review the performance of his secretary yearly at one firm. There was a budget set aside for taking the secretaries out of the office (neutral ground) and many just used to take them to the chain coffee shop next door. His secretary was a woman of wisdom, and taste. She used to ask to be taken for Afternoon Tea at a nearby posh hotel. It still came in on budget, but the whole experience was elevated from a chore to a ritual just by upping the venue.

Look at the rituals your office has, or doesn't have. Do you have routines in place for managing emails? For dealing with the post? For communicating significant dates?

Making your email time sacred can be as easy as shutting the door, setting a timer and letting everyone know that for that half hour you NEED to work undisturbed. Likewise, tidying your desk daily ready for the next day can be a ritual that you make clear you need to do. In pure Simple Abundance[17] terms, you would light a candle, sip at a chai latte and clear it holistically, but in real terms you will probably be glugging down cold coffee, making piles of files into larger piles and wondering why the desk never seems to be made of wood these days.

Use the things you do every day to ground you. Find a tea you like. Make the afternoon tea break a moment of calm, taking the few minutes it takes to boil the water and pour it over the loose tea or teabag (depending on how High ritual you want to be) as an oasis of thought. Consciously empty your mind of anything but that moment. I'm useless at emptying my mind: I need to fill it with something else, and find that by telling yourself what you are doing, "I am filling the kettle. I am waiting for the water to boil. I am filling the cup..." you do actually put yourself in the moment. Now, that's where

---

[17] Simple Abundance was a book back in the late 90's. Its basic aim was to add beauty, grace and love to our lives, and to make the world a better place through the care we took of ourselves. https://www.goodreads.com/book/show/748862.Simple_Abundance

mindfulness stops, but with hygge you can make this a moment of appreciation as well, "I am enjoying the sound of running water as I fill the kettle: I love the smell of the chai tea as I fill my cup. I am glad that I can have milk..."

I love schools, because they're full of children and children, especially younger ones, love a bit of ritual. The best part of the day for me as a teacher was Hometime, when you'd get the children sorted with coats, bags, paper, and then if you were a sensible teacher read a story. The children went home with pictures floating through their mind and smiles very often on their faces after a happy day. I'm not saying to have a story time at work, but a sharing time with work colleagues can be a great thing. Just taking a minute or two to ask someone else about their day and share the good and the bad about it can be a centring activity.

Building rituals into the day takes time, and continued effort, but wouldn't it feel better to know that you have a bright spot waiting for you at 2pm? Or 5pm? Or that a mundane task has been made better by thinking about it and adding an extra touch of humanity?

6. **Every member of staff is valuable**:
Equality is an important feature of the Danish society. All citizens have equal rights and all are valued members of society. That's an idealistic point of view,

and in cynical Britain we may argue that they are just saying it rather than living it, but we should be looking at our traditional hierarchical structure and wondering if we're guilty of putting too much emphasis on the few at the top, rather than truly making work and life an equally beneficial experience for all.

You have the chance to show how equality works. If you're a boss, don't always expect an underling to make you tea or coffee, if you're an underling, watch and think if there are things that can be improved upon to the benefit of all. Never be afraid to raise a point that you need clarified, and always carry the certainty that the most important people to have on your side in a school are the Caretaker and Cleaner. That might be so in an office as well, I don't altogether know.

Make sure that all members of staff are involved in hyggely moments (or at least all members of staff in your immediate vicinity: if you work for a large company your team may well be the people on your floor, or the large office space you work in. It's up to you to define your team) but if it comes to things like cake, then also make sure that there is some left over for the people who clean up after you. Leave it with a note of thanks, and hope they have a hyggely moment themselves at the end of the day!

7. **Learn to decompress and leave work in the workplace**.

It's no use having a high-powered job full of stress and taking that stress home to blast at the family. That's a recipe for tears, recriminations and a bad atmosphere in the home. Far better to learn how to destress before you get into the house. This is where a commute of any length helps. You can use that time to get rid of the negative feelings of the day, to start to anticipate the evening ahead and to make a distinct cut off between work and home. Or, if you must bring work home, you can create a calm atmosphere to work in.

Train or bus travel is useful. Being able to read a book or to listen to podcasts means you can associate the journey with something pleasant. I love the Kindle app on my phone: I'm never without something to read. And Audible do a great line in audiobooks. They can be listened to even in the car, so any commute becomes a chance to learn.

Perhaps you could use part of your commute as exercise. Getting off early and walking part of the route could easily help you achieve the recommended target of 10,000 steps a day, while foregoing lifts and walking every set of stairs available also helps. In the car, try bottom tightening exercises whenever you're at a set of traffic lights, or parking a few streets away.

I always arrive late at the office, but I make up for it by leaving early.

Charles Lamb

www.howtohyggethebritishway.com

If you don't have a commute, or you work from home, then finding time to destress is much harder, but not impossible. You will need an at-home ritual to centre you after work. Perhaps, when the day is done, you could have a shower or a bath, change into comfortable clothes or make a tea break when you consciously say, "This is the end of my working day."

8. **Sometimes the stresses are too much to leave behind in a simple way**.

At times like this, you will need to find a strategy that makes moving on easier. Could you write down all your worries in a notebook? Do you have a friend who would listen to your concerns and be useful? Identify what it is that is stressing you, and try to identify what you can do about it. Sometimes there is no easy solution, but being able to rationalise your stress and either work through it or work it out helps. Never be afraid to ask for help if the stresses are really too much to bear. Better to ask for help than collapse under the strain.

9. **Appreciate the joy of a warm cuppa**. I asked the Hygge Nookworms what they thought belonged in a hyggely office.

   They're always so good for suggestions. Here are a few of their answers, plus *the* top quote from one member.

   - Plants on the desk. Several members suggested this. They also kept fish on their desks (in a goldfish bowl, of course!).
   - Natural objects scored highly. One lady said that she had "Lake Superior rocks on my desk as well as a tiny Japanese sand box with a tiny rake". I have a rock on my desk at the moment. I collected it on holiday, meaning to paint it, but it reminds me that there is a big world beyond the office walls!

- Lamps to suit you. Overhead fluorescent lighting is not the best for thinking by. Especially when they start to flicker. Salt lamps also got mentioned as a way of increasing negative ions in the air. I could imagine a good reading lamp, positioned to avoid screen flare, would be a very good addition to an office.

- Fake candles. Real ones are likely to be banned on Health and Safety grounds, but a fake candle can give you the glow on a Winter's evening, just enough to warm the cockles of your heart.

- A lovely smell. There are diffusers that plug into a usb port on your computer and let you scent your air with whichever fragrance you desire. You can also get electric wax burners that will melt scented wax and diffuse the fragrance into the air.

- Decent drinks. The Nookworms liked decent coffee and some like loose-leaf tea. They might sound extravagant, but both are available at a good price from the supermarket.

- Treats. Chocolate topped the advice list here, but cake also got many mentions as a hyggely thing to have.

- A good view. If you can't make it, fake it. If your office has no decent view through a window, then find a lovely piece of artwork that you can display, or just a screensaver that makes you smile. A view out over mountains or waterfalls can help you relax, and relaxation is part of hygge, isn't it?

And for the ultimate office envy, listen to this description of one Nookworm's office:

I am lucky enough to have a private office with a window. I don't use the overhead lighting. I brought in lamps, plants, photos and some pretty hand me down art on the walls. A co-worker gave me a table-top fountain and I have shells on my desk from my beach vacation. I play classical piano music on my computer and a scented wax warmer. The first thing I do every morning is turn everything on and enjoy a cup of tea in my special mug to get ready for the day. My job can be very stressful so this puts me in a good frame of mind. I get lots of comments on how soothing my office is.

3: Hygge With Your Family

Families are wonderful things, aren't they? A group of people, often with very different viewpoints or interests, who are thrown together by the whims of genetic lottery and told from being young that because they happen to share a surname and a lot of their DNA is similar, that they have a mythical bond that is deeper than the one they share with their friends. Or was that just my childhood?

Certainly, there is a bit of the Dickens about families, they can be the best of times or the worst of times. The people who love you enough to buy you your favourite chocolate are also the ones who know you well enough to know what words hurt. In real life you won't get a happy, hyggely family most of the time. However, that doesn't mean you can't do your best to try. If you've got a young family you'll be building memories that, good or bad, shape the adult your child will be, while those with older children or adult children will be spending precious time together that grows increasingly more precious as time goes by.

The ideas here may not be age appropriate for every family. Like everything else in this book, what screams hygge to your family may be completely different from what hygge means to mine. Read, assimilate, isolate the golden nuggets and chuck away the rest. You aren't aiming for an advert-perfect family, just a family that plays together well most of the time.

There is no doubt that it is around the family and the home that all the greatest virtues, the most dominating virtues of human society, are created, strengthened and maintained

Winston Churchill (via Hygge Jem)

1. Slow down together.

In this uber-competitive world it is easy for many families to be forever busy, to have so many things going on after school that weeknights turn into roundabouts as one member comes in and another goes out. Schoolchildren, especially, seem to fall victim to the do-everything-and-do-it-all-at-once approach.

But if the amount of activities being done by the family is interfering with the family eating together, or spending time together, then it's having an adverse effect on family life. Far better to slow down and be choosy about what you do. Our children, when they were younger, were told they could only take part in two after-school activities, and, please, only one in the evenings. We wanted to be able to eat together as a family almost every night, if possible.

The children accepted this limitation and chose carefully. If they found a new activity they liked the sound of, they had to choose carefully between that and an older one. At one time, it did mean we were still taxiing three different children to three different groups on three different nights: but we weren't doing all three every night. I'd like to think they are still very picky about how they spend their time now, and that family time is still crucial to them.

2. **Learn to embrace the weather.**

So often we stay in when the weather turns cold or wet. In Denmark, Germany and all over the continent where the weather can be bitter, they have a saying, "There's no bad weather, only the wrong clothes." Be prepared with decent waterproofs or an umbrella that you'll want to use, so that when the rain falls and everybody else looks askance, you can whip out your brolly and walk proudly in the rain!

Getting children to wear waterproofs can be a hard job: let them choose their own mac, wellies or brolly. I know when I was 3 my favourite shoes were a pair of red knee high boots, bought for me to wear in the cold weather that year. I kept them by my bed and put them on every day I possibly could. They were good value, I must have worn them every day until they were too little for me, when my Mum had to hide them away from me! Sometimes tantrums can also be avoided by having multiple sets of clothes to choose from. "Will you wear your *Peppa Pig* coat or your *In The Night Garden* waterproof?" might be enough of a choice for a toddler to make and still keep dry on the way to the shops. In the end, remember there are very few days in this country when they'll catch much if they go out hatless, gloveless or with no coat on.

And don't forget that having been out in the weather, part of the hygge of the thing is the coming home again. If you can, put slippers or hygge-socks on a radiator to warm while you're out and hang wet things to dry ready for next time. You can even create a mud-room with bench and hooks to make a feature of them!

3. **Get outside as often as possible.**

When my children were little, going for long walks in the local park or woods was an adventure. Even on days when we didn't have the time for a big adventure, getting out with the tricycles or ride along toys gave us a breath of fresh air and helped to tire them out for the evening.

And in the Summer, an afternoon of relentless heat could be cooled by getting water pistols out and having

Jo Kneale

fights in the garden. We also used to enjoy watering the garden with the hose, and playing in the water.

Nowadays, we get outside in the evenings, but after we've watered any plants we're more likely to sit around the fire-pit swapping stories and enjoying a cool drink in the late summer evening light. I found that so valuable when my sons were doing GCSEs and A levels, because a teenage boy very often will talk about things when sat staring into the flames of a fire when getting a hello out of him in ordinary circumstances is like blood out of a stone! And there is something so magical about sipping cider from the bottle as the last golden rays of sunshine pass over head.

4. **Remember hygge will be different for every family.**

I have friends who love camping. I mean LOVE camping. Their Mum runs a forest school, so being outside, lighting fires, finding foliage and traipsing around in the undergrowth is very much part of her DNA. The family of 5 pack up almost every school holidays and go camping. Not even caravanning with a toilet and shower block to hand, but proper old-style camping, with outside loo if you're lucky and a tap in the middle to provide the water. It's very Famous Five and they love it. For them, sitting around the campfire with their scalded tea and singing to a gently strummed guitar is hygge.

My boys would leave after one night.

They've tried it, they didn't like it. Our hygge would be playing Settlers of Catan or Risk around the table after a good tea, or an afternoon in the cinema watching some movie or other, or sitting round after a lovely meal on holiday and just talking. In fact, a lot of our hygge involves food and TV, since we regularly make a cake just especially to watch during whatever Sunday night drama series is on. And when they were little, family hygge often involved a steam engine of one sort or another. It's just what we like. I love crafting and art as a hobby, so I'm happy sitting and crocheting, while David reads and James plays on the computer, Sarah chooses the TV show and Peter (husband) sleeps.

We're altogether in the same room, swapping stories, enjoying just being together.

The activity is to an extent immaterial, what's more important is the feeling of peace, togetherness, security that we have. Find out what ticks the most boxes for your family, and do that.

Be aware that there will be days when for one reason or another the hyggely feeling doesn't happen, and that some days you might be better off just taking one member of the family aside to bond with. That happens especially if your children have very diverse interests. If one, say, is an engineer and loves the science museum while the other espouses books and all things literary, then taking them together would guarantee a day when one of them should be disappointed. Either find common ground or, and I find this works best, take them separately.

You will find, especially as children grow into young adults, that time spent with them doing what they want is a memory to treasure. You do have to be prepared to look eager when they show you the piston or explain why Manga and Anime are related, but not the same.

5. **Make every member of the family responsible for keeping the house tidy enough to enjoy hygge.**

Learning to work around the house together is a good introduction to real life, as well as giving the child responsibility for something.

In my house, each person has their own special area that they are good at cleaning (well, good-enough at cleaning) so for example, my second son cleans the downstairs loo when we have the mad dash to get the place habitable, while both the eldest son and the daughter have got good at cleaning out the guinea pigs and then cleaning up after the clean-out.

And when we all work together, the relaxation afterwards is very hyggely. There are few pleasures to compare to leaning back in a clean room and smelling the polish before sharing a biscuit or slice of cake with your fellow workers.

You could use Pinterest or the internet as a source of ideas for chore charts to start using when your children are younger. Yes, it is work and, yes, it isn't very exciting, but build in a reward in at the end and do your best. Sitting in a clean room eating lemon drizzle cake after working hard on the house that afternoon is a great reward.

6. **Create special routines and rituals to build in hyggely moments to the day.**

With younger children, these routines are just obvious: bedtime, bath time, bedtime story all fall naturally into space. Even during daylight hours little children have a need for naptime and snack time, which builds in rest and relaxation to their day. Oh, to be able to keep those routines into adulthood!

Well, truthfully, until about 20 years ago the routines of rest were still part of life. Break-times, lunchtimes, afternoon tea break were all part of office work. It was the go-get them 80s that did for it! In an era when lunch was for wimps, productivity became king and breaks were an imposition. I think we lose out when we don't accept that human bodies, children and adults, need to pause and to stop for a few minutes.

Stop and look at your life at the moment. When are the natural pauses in your life? I have three teenagers and there seems to be a natural break just after they come in from school and I arrive home from work and before the rush to start cooking dinner begins. I wish I could say we sit and eat homemade cookies and milk every day. Ha. We don't, because I work full time, but we do sit together in the living room while the kids eat toast or whatever biscuits were in the tin and I sip a cup of tea.

After dinner is also another natural pause. The older the children get (and they are really young adults now) the better they are at staying longer over the table and talking. Sometimes these evenings spontaneously burst out into a games session or a challenge to complete a quiz. I love these evenings especially when they aren't at school and you can see them relax, with no homework to rush off to.

We have guinea pigs that live in the living room. They need daily care, so getting together to clean them out happens every night at about 10 o'clock. It sounds strange, but actually working together for the good of the piggies is a great feeling of hygge. Sometimes hygge isn't just being selfishly lazy, but actively good for others.

Rituals are slightly different from routines, in that they are more mindful, ask for greater involvement by the participants and create a sense of belonging.

Rituals with a family can include such simple things as lighting the Advent Candles in the countdown to Christmas, sharing breakfast as a special time on a Saturday or the rituals you choose to celebrate birthdays with.

Rituals are easier to adopt when the children are younger and happy to go along with what you're asking them to do, but it's possible to develop a small ritual as the years go by and still have it in place when the kids become adults. Our Christmas morning is a ritual: small stocking upstairs on Mum and Dad's bed, before coming downstairs for the Big Presents. God knows how we fit 5 adult-sized people on the one bed, but we do.

Will the ritual change? Yes, as the children mature, of course it will. But we'll replace it with other rituals.

7. **Eat together as often as possible.**

Yes, I know you've just swallowed your teeth and are fuming about Middle Class families with an unreasonable expectation of dinnertimes spent around the table and talking over Tarquin's day…. But hear me out. Eating together has proven benefits in terms of health, mind and intelligence[18] but even without those benefits, it's still a very good chance to pin your family down without the distraction of phone and/or TV and try to get a conversation going. We don't allow phones or books at the table (good job, or I'd never talk to them) and the kids are assiduous in making sure I keep to my own rules.

Over the years we've had some of the best talks at the dinner table. Somehow, eating together encourages sharing. Problems at school, issues with homework, a worry that was niggling them; they've all shared stuff over the lasagne that would have taken torture to extract any other way. Like watching a fire, eating is a distraction that seems to help the child open up.

Involving the child in preparing the food is also a good chance to feel more hyggely. If they know the time and

---

[18]   https://www.theatlantic.com/health/archive/2014/07/the-importance-of-eating-together/374256/

effort needed to make a meal, they should appreciate it more than if the meal appears as if by magic. And cooking is a valuable life skill to learn. I have two children who will happily cook a meal from scratch, and I'm working on the third. They cook the meals they learned to cook alongside me, and probably would freak at just being asked to cook anything, but they prove helpful when I need to get something on the table ready by a certain time and I've been delayed elsewhere.

I do try to involve them in planning the meals. Usually I sit with my list of family favourite meals and a blank sheet, dated for a whole month. I work out what we're up to on different days and what time is available for cooking. Then we try to come up with meals that suit the day according to who will be cooking and how long we have to cook. I won't do a stew on a day when we have half an hour and several people out pronto, whereas a quick stir fry would be ideal. And I always make sure I have an emergency meal in the store cupboard or freezer that is both quick and easy in case I need it.

8. **Fika is not just for the Office**.
Breaking mid-morning or mid-afternoon for a little treat is a wonderful opportunity to feel hyggely with the family.

I think we need to build pauses into life again. The Swedes famously have Fika, both a noun and a verb, meaning to pause over a cake and a cup of tea. It's not possible every day, I know, but it should be something we could do twice a week, say, when we stop and share a cake or biscuits. During the week perhaps it could be more of an afternoon tea, a plate of biscuits or toast after school and work and before any activities that we race off to.

At the weekend, it would be wonderful sometimes to put a morning aside and have a Fika break: cake, drinks and a gathering of the household just to stop and share time together. It wouldn't be fair if the only people we shared a cake treat with were the people we work with.

One of our favourite cakes recently has been Kladdkaka, the Swedish cake that really is squishy and like eating raw cake mix. It's messy, but so worth it!

We have a family tradition of tea and cake during certain drama series. Downton Abbey used to work well for that. Sipping Chai Tea from teacups and delicately nibbling lemon drizzle or Victoria sponge while Lady Violet delivered one of her put-downs was a highlight of the week. As a family, we're all watching Game of Thrones, but somehow it doesn't have the same vibe. I rather think we should be drinking mead and chewing on a meat bone after the roast instead. Mmm. Matching

Fika to the programme we're watching has possibilities.... Poldark with cider and apple cake; Gilmore Girls accompanied by coffee and pizza. The Killing helped along by traditional Scandinavian cinnamon buns. Think where the programme is set and what food is served there. The possibilities are endless.

9. **Plan a hyggely party carefully.**

As a veteran of many family parties for birthdays, Christmas and other special occasions, I can tell you that planning a party carefully is important. Not, I mean, that you plan to the minute, or even plan every aspect intimately, but that you consider who is coming and whether they make a good mix. Part of the secret of hygge is that everybody should feel relaxed and safe enough to talk freely. If you know that you have two siblings who rip strips off each other whenever they meet, then it may be more diplomatic to have them separated for some parties, or to have parties so big that there's a good chance they won't kick off.

Families need to consider the timing of parties to suit the children involved. Birthday parties for a one-year-old that take up nap time are never popular: either the child gripes all the time, or is asleep and you can guarantee they will sleep longer than ever and spoil the fun!

And the size of the party can make a big difference. When my extended family meet up there are well over 20 people just looking at my brothers, sisters-in-law and nieces and nephews. With a family that big it's difficult sometimes to speak to everybody and the person throwing the party may never get out of the kitchen!

The older I get, the less I feel inclined to spend that time alone. My parties have become easier affairs, with a massive pot of chilli or curry or Bolognese, and everybody helps themselves. Much better. Or I keep the group to less than 10, and know that whoever comes will help in the preparation and clean up as well.

10.   **Outdoors Hygge is Good for you all**.

If you haven't got space outside, of any sort, then find a place nearby where you can sit. With young children… or even with older ones… finding the local park that is most child-friendly may be your best bet. We have several parks within walking distance, but at least one of them is no use for playing on because of dog walkers.

Fortunately, our local park in Liverpool, Calderstones, is a very family-friendly park, with play areas for younger children and adventure areas for older, a café, an ice cream shop and a Storybarn. It's been taken on by a wonderful organisation called The Reader [19]and they

75

run all sorts of events there through the year. It was always a favourite Sunday stroll when the kids were little and is still a favourite haunt now they're older.

On a summer Sunday, you can see lots of people out with their picnics, blankets spread out and settled under a tree so that they can stay there for the afternoon. Outdoor living made easy.

Look online for events in parks that will give you an idea of which one to choose. Ask on Facebook as well, since friends may have found a little gem that nobody else knows about.

11. The family that plays together stays together.

Since the kids were small we have had board games in the house. Actually, board games come into their own when the child hits about 10 and learns the strategies they need to win. Before then we had great arguments about why rules really mattered.

I think young children need to learn to play games precisely because learning to stick to rules is a valuable life skill, while learning how to apply the strategy and bend the rules to suit is an even more valuable one. Start early, persist and keep looking for the perfect games for your family. We love the more risqué adult-aged games now, like Exploding Kittens, Cards Against

---

[19] http://www.thereader.org.uk/

Humanity or Kittens in a Blender. Basically anything rude or violent.

Settlers of Catan is another family favourite. We only have the four player version, and five people in the family, so buying an extension pack is on my list of things to do.

But back when the children were little we had the classics like Monopoly, Cluedo and Mousetrap. They still come out now and again, especially if we have guests with younger children. And is there anything more hyggely to do on a cold, wet, winter's Saturday than switch off the lights and play card games by candlelight?

12. **Holidays are Hygge memory-making sessions**.

Going away on holiday is one of my most stressful things to organise each year. That's because I'm the list maker, the organiser, the thinker for me and the children. I have been able to delegate more over the years, but when you're still the one saying "Remember the toothbrush and have you packed extra socks?" to three kids and one husband, it gets to be a pain. Fortunately, I have a very short memory and once on holiday I hit relaxed mode well.

Our holidays tend to be self-catering. We made that decision early in our life as parents, when the cost and effort needed to stay in a hotel with even one child became clear. We liked having a place to sit and relax after the babies had gone to bed. Now we like having space to sit and relax with the young adults we're raising. Either way, self-catering gives you the space to make use of.

Because of their very nature, holidays should be a good chance to hygge with the family. No work, plenty of time together, usually a lovely area to visit nearby, and that holiday feeling that means rules are relaxed and long evenings spent chatting and drinking coke aren't going to lead to tears before school the next day.

I know the state of the accommodation can vary, and that the travel can be stressful, but take time out of any incidents and problems to appreciate the moment. Encourage the children to pause and enjoy the food, or the view, or just the fact that they are on a beach, in a park, in a museum, staying in a different place.

Build in possible hygge by packing picnics for the zoo, finding a good ice cream shop nearby, looking for activities that suit everyone. Our last holiday in Wales was beautifully hyggely most days, with afternoon tea at an NT house for me, go-karting for two of my children and long afternoons sat reading on or off the beach for my bookworm husband and eldest son.

When our children were young we also used to visit the same three houses for several years in a row. We had the 'Upside Down House', the 'House With No Stairs' and the 'House With A View'. Because they'd been before and knew where they were going, the children could settle in straight away, get their stuff out and start enjoying the craic without the looking round or wondering where they were bit. We still visit one of the houses (borrowed off family) and it's like settling into a real home-from-home when we do.

If the accommodation isn't feeling homey, then add some touches to help you. Most places I stay usually put flowers in a vase somewhere, but if they haven't then you could buy a small bunch and pop them in glasses in the living room and kitchen. Keep a loaded fruit bowl out, or spread your magazines, toys, crafts or colouring out and make yourself at home.

I also find smell helps me to feel settled in, so I'm a great one for taking a scented candle or two with me. I love rose geranium, and I appreciate a citronella candle to light on any patio area we sit on. Small votives don't take up a lot of space, and can be reasonably priced as well. I do actually know someone who takes her own family photo away so that, for the time they're there, the place is absolutely theirs. I'm not that mad. Yet.

Holidays are ideal chances to indulge in fika as well. You'll usually find yourself so hungry mid-afternoon that a break for cake or ice cream is the most sensible thing to do. Try to find cosy tea rooms or independent bakeries where the offering will be different from the usual. National Trust tearooms can be pricey but often delicious. And as a last resort, take some stuff and make your own.

One of my favourite books is Warning of Gales[20] by Annie Sanders. I read this every year just for the description of how Imogen prepares and packs for the holiday, and the little vignettes of eating Cornish pasties with milk. Imogen packs everything… and even contemplates taking her KitchenAid. Yes, really. It's a good chick lit book.

13. **Seasonal routines underpin hygge**.

This should be obvious, really. The activities that build up hygge in the summer and the activities that make winter hyggely will be different.

In the summer, you should expect to be outdoors, enjoying the sunshine, visiting places on holiday and enjoying the fruits of the summer. Ice cream will probably feature strongly along with finding ways to keep cool.

In the wintertime, hygge may be more about indoors hygge, with the emphasis on time together around the table, games or TV as a centring activity, crafts and reading by candlelight.

It's useful to mark the seasons of the year by the festivals. Whether you're religious or not, there are festivals or feast days to celebrate that mark off the beginning of spring, the middle of summer, the end of

---

[20] https://www.amazon.co.uk/Warnings-Gales-Annie-Sanders-ebook/dp/B003NUSC0O/ref=sr_1_1_twi_kin_2?ie=UTF8&qid=1488543234&sr=8-1&keywords=warning+of+gales

the holidays, the start of darkness in Autumn time and the middle of winter.

I found a couple of books useful in the early days of motherhood, *All Year Round: a calendar of celebrations*[21] by Fynes-Clinton, Rowling and Druitt and *Festivals, Family and Food* by Diana Carey and Judy Large[22]. Both books had stories and crafts connected to most festivals of the British Isles, including a few that are less well known.

I also loved *Mrs Sharp's Traditions: Reviving Victorian Celebrations* by Sarah Ban Breathnach[23]. Sadly out of print now, this book had various quaint ideas for celebrating throughout the year.

It was good to look beyond the usual annual festivals and to find ideas for making Spring or Autumn equinox more of an occasion. There are other annual celebration books around, or why not look to other traditions to build up a set of rituals for your family.

14. Finally, Christmas: Peak Hygge Season!!

[21]   https://www.amazon.co.uk/d/cka/All-Year-Round-Calendar-Celebrations-Festivals-Seasons/1869890477/ref=sr_1_7?ie=UTF8&qid=1488544302&sr=8-7&keywords=a+year+of+festivals

[22]   https://www.amazon.co.uk/Festivals-Family-Food-Judy-Large/dp/095070623X/ref=pd_bxgy_14_2?_encoding=UTF8&psc=1&refRID=J0E32YR5DFGAY3M443YG

[23]   https://www.amazon.co.uk/d/Books/Mrs-Sharps-Traditions-Reviving-Victorian-Celebrations-Comfort/074321076X/ref=sr_1_11?s=books&ie=UTF8&qid=1488544539&sr=1-11&keywords=sarah+ban+breathnach

No look at hygge in the family would be complete without talking about the Hygge Highlight of the year. The time of the year when mothers all over the world stress about the decorations, the food, the full calendar, the food, the clothes, the food, getting the house clean, the food, keeping it clean, the food and where Aunt Agatha is going to sleep because she has a bad back and can't have the camp-bed that everybody else sleeps on and Oh God will she want driving home at 8pm on Christmas Day and who on earth will stay sober enough to drive her??? And the food.

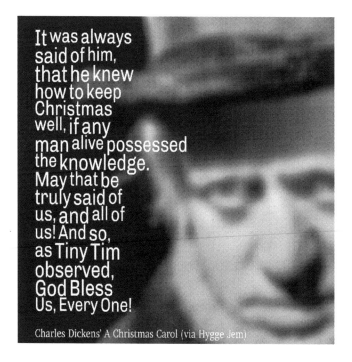

It was always said of him, that he knew how to keep Christmas well, if any man alive possessed the knowledge. May that be truly said of us, and all of us! And so, as Tiny Tim observed, God Bless Us, Every One!

Charles Dickens' A Christmas Carol (via Hygge Jem)

Christmas is one of the most stressful times of year, let's be truthful. The expectations placed on us by magazines, memories and the effort of paying for it using only one month's pay packet (or face paying for it on credit for the next 17 years) are immense. How can it be the season of hygge?

Well, here I say let's learn from the Danes. Christmas is what we want it to be, and it doesn't have to cost the Earth or bankrupt our wallets.

I could go into the details here of setting up budgets, lowering costs, examining what events mean Christmas to you and jettisoning some of those that are done from duty alone rather than the expectation of joy. I won't, because that would take up so much space in the book and you would be so asleep at the end. How to Hygge Your Christmas The British Way would make a book all by itself!! (mmm…. Good idea… let me write it down…).

Instead, let me concentrate on the hyggely parts. Which is to say, remember that your tribe will help you celebrate Christmas best. Who do you want to spend Christmas with really? And what do you need to do to make that happen?

A few years ago our Christmas Days were spent with an elderly relative on Peter's side of the family. He came to us, bringing gifts, and had lunch, and a watch of the children playing before beautifully asking at 5pm prompt could we take him home. When he died, we began to get together with my brothers and sisters-in-law and all the nieces and nephews.

There were over 20 of us, all in one room, trying to have Christmas Dinner altogether. It didn't feel hyggely to me, it was loud and raucous and it gave me a headache and I longed for the time to have my own smaller dinner with my tribe. Don't get me wrong, I love my brothers and there are times when parties with them are fun, but Christmas Day was just becoming a chore, a duty.

For the past couple of years we have been home again, with my parents who are now the elderly relatives, or alone just the five of us. We eat at a time that suits us, have a hyggely day full of laughter and rest. We play games, watch Christmas TV, eat too much food, drink too much alcohol, have a house full of paper and boxes for a while and then collapse, exhausted, for an early night.

Take a piece of paper now and jot down what you remember from last year or the year before... just a list, not an essay. Now put a star next to your must-do items. These are the things that spark joy for you or the family and that would be missed if you didn't do them. The church service, the visit to Santa, having the neighbours around for mulled wine. These are the Lego bricks of your Christmas. Everything else you do will be built on them.

Your Christmas full of hygge will be one that suits you. I daren't presume to dictate what you should do and with whom. Think about the things you have planned, and concentrate on making them more hyggely. Do you need more friends? Less? Time to relax? A visit to other people? Do you need to concentrate on having a frugal Christmas so that money worries don't ruin your hygge vibe?

Some time spent planning in advance, even during the summer when Christmas hasn't yet reared its head, will pay dividends in creating a happy, hygge-full time.

4: Hygge For The Soul

Making space in your soul to feel happy can sometimes take no more than a kind thought about yourself. Certainly, friends I know who have suffered from SAD or mild depression say that it isn't until they take care of themselves with the same degree of love that they take care of others that they make proper improvements. We are all so busy looking after others, people or things, that remembering to give ourselves credit or take a break can be hard.

I like the oxygen mask analogy. When the plane crashes, care-givers are under strict instructions to put on their own oxygen masks before looking after those in their charge. In other words, if we don't take care of our own survival, we're really endangering not only ourselves but those we have responsibility for.

Meik Wiking's favourite description of hygge is as "cocoa by candlelight" but he also likes "cosiness for the soul". Hygge should leave us feeling cared for, whether by other people or by ourselves. This chapter has a few simple ideas for treating yourself well, for spending time hyggering alone and for becoming even more aware of the things that make you happy.

1. **Appreciation plays a large part in making you happy**.

   Research shows that people who keep a gratitude journal can have improved sleep patterns, better scores at school, succeed in their goals more often… as well as actually feeling happier. You can read through some of the research in this Psychology Today article, The Benefits of Adding Gratitude to your Attitude. Added to that, having a list of things that make you feel happy will give you a bolster on days when it's all grey and miserable out there. Why not grab a small notebook, or set a page aside in your planner, and just jot down the things that have tickled you? Although recording every day sounds ideal, research suggests that even as few times as once a week will have an impact and may be more realistic. At Christmas 2016, one of the big sellers was actually a 5 year journal big enough only for one sentence a day.

2. **Find your tribe**. We all have one.

   Somewhere out there will be a group of people who like what you like. If you can't find a physical tribe, find a virtual one.

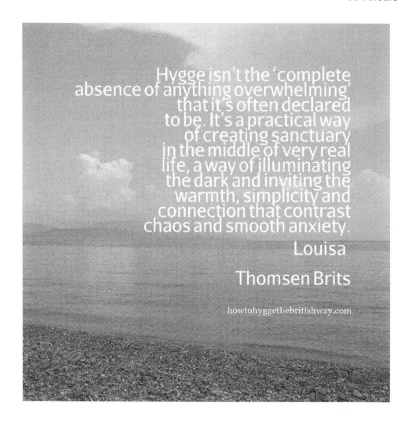

Hygge isn't the 'complete absence of anything overwhelming' that it's often declared to be. It's a practical way of creating sanctuary in the middle of very real life, a way of illuminating the dark and inviting the warmth, simplicity and connection that contrast chaos and smooth anxiety.

Louisa Thomsen Brits

howtohyggethebritishway.com

When I was growing up, crafts like knitting and crochet were… well, they hadn't come back into fashion, so I struggled to find anybody who would validate the things I liked to spend my time on. I grew up tribeless as a teenager and into early adulthood. It probably wasn't until I had my first child, and the internet was cheap enough to be easily available at home, that I realised there were people out there who also knitted and sewed and that, for the sake of sitting and writing a post now and again, I could communicate with them.

Facebook makes finding a tribe even easier, since there is probably a group for whatever you are in to or, if there isn't, starting your own group is easy.

I belong to several crochet groups. Some recipe sharing groups and, of course, a couple of Hygge groups. One of these I started myself in October 2016 with 10 friends and the intention of creating a caring, sharing space where people could explore hygge without judgement or competition. I love it, and if you're reading this book the chances are you'd love it, too![24]

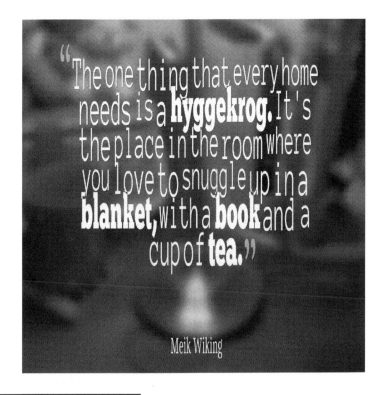

"The one thing that every home needs is a **hyggekrog.** It's the place in the room where you love to snuggle up in a **blanket,** with a **book** and a cup of **tea.**"

Meik Wiking

---

[24] The link is https://www.facebook.com/groups/TheHyggeNook/ Everyone is welcome, and we have a very happy atmosphere.

I took the name from Meik Wiking's advice that everybody needs a Hyggekrog, a Hygge Nook, to call their own.

3. **Collect memories not things.**

It took me years to realise that I didn't need the champagne cork from every celebration bottle I'd ever opened. In fact, after the first 3 you can't remember which was which and why you have it anyway, so much better never to keep them in the first place.

It was the same with souvenirs from the souvenir shop. Why did I feel the need to have a piece of tat with the name of a place on it? Who needs a pot saying Skegness? Or a Chatsworth paper weight?? I must have bought, and subsequently offloaded a pile of stuff I neither needed nor really wanted. Now I might buy a postcard if I haven't been able to take a good photo, but usually the only thing I buy from the shop is a cup of tea.

4. **Step away from the camera.**

Again, this was a good lesson for me to learn. I don't print out the pictures I take or put them on display. I don't usually share family photos on the internet, and yet I could happily spend hours watching everything through the lens of my phone rather than being there.

Is that hygge? No! Much better to watch with both eyes, then discuss afterwards to keep the memory. It's why I'm a great one for posting quotes on Instagram. I'm too busy enjoying to stage photos.

And in a fantastic touch of hypocrisy, I love looking at other people's photographs. Perhaps I don't have a good eye for photography, but mine never do look as professional. I really do point, shoot and run... usually in that order, but not always!

5. **Find a pub or a cafe and make it your local**.

Not that you'll be getting drunk in there often. This is a place outside of the house that you can embrace as your hygge nook. Choose one for the atmosphere and the seating.

Good lighting helps, by which I mean, of course, lighting that is gentle and not harsh, allowing the age of the females in your party to remain delicately unknowable. If you have particular tastes in alcohol (real beer, flavoured gin) then keep looking to find the right place that suits you. Then visit. Often enough to feel happy when you walk in.

That takes a bit of time, but every other week or at least once a month for a year should help. It's easier if the pub or cafe is within walking distance, and you know other people who go there. The aim is to be well enough known that you walk in and they smile hello, not so well known that you walk in and they get your drink ready.

Have a regular weekly slot when you drop in for a drink or a hot drink, have a favourite hot drink and have a favourite few seats that you know give you a good view of the world going by.

A café that is a short walk from work can also be good if you use it during lunchtimes. The atmosphere matters here as well. You can get hyggely in a chain café (indeed, the comfy chairs and subdued lighting are designed specifically to get you and keep you) but it can be good to find your own private café, an owner-run café where staff turnover is low and you can build a rapport with them.

Shy of going to a pub or café alone? Then look at the noticeboard. Some cafes run stitch and bitch or book club sessions, when going in alone won't be so intimidating. Or ask a close friend and set up a regular date to meet over a coffee.

I have no trouble being alone in a café, I take my book, Kindle or notebook and always have plenty to do to be alone. Or I watch people. I love people watching.

6. **Appreciate the joy of a warm cup of tea when you come inside from the cold or wet**.

It's a joke in our house that the first thing that gets switched on when we get in is the kettle. There are very few physical ailments caused by walking in the rain that can't be cured by a warm shower and a hot cuppa.

If tea's not your thing, find a hot drink that is. Coffee, hot chocolate or even hot water can all warm you up on a cold day. My children used to be partial to tomato soup, only ever Heinz, heated and drunk from a mug on really cold, dark, damp days or after snow.

Investing in a lovely big mug, ½ pint sized, gives enough space to hold a decent amount and allow for hands wrapped well around it. The provenance of the mug doesn't really matter, there are no benefits to be gained from a hand-thrown limited edition as opposed to a mass-produced supermarket's own brand, so long as it holds heat well and suits you.

The tea or coffee needn't be expensive either.... Builder's tea works just as well. I have a fondness for a certain supermarket's own brand of chai. It's far cheaper than many more exotic kinds, but in terms of flavour and spiciness hits the spot for me every time.

7. **Use your support system to build in happiness**.

This is simple: get out with your friends. Hygge can happen alone, but shared hygge is better. If you live alone, you need the support of others around you. Go find a club, join a group, ask a friend to tea. Go make contact and spend time with others. You need physical contact and emotional support to be at your best.

Part of keeping hygge in your soul is making sure the hygge is there. Try the Women's Institute, or a craft, musical or sports group in your area. Ask a friend or colleague for ideas. And if the group you want doesn't exist, then start one. I started my bookclub because I wanted to be a member. I'm thinking of starting a hygge circle, meeting once a month to share food & ideas.

8. **Take hygge out to others**.

   You can say more in a smile and a quick touch of the hand than in a lecture. If you're in need of hygge, take that hygge to someone who can't get out. Adopt a granny, visit a mother of many children under 4 years old, grab your neighbour who lives alone and get out.

   Build a friendship with them and make the time you spend together peak hygge growing ground. It might not always happen, but if the opportunity is there, there is an increased chance that the two of you will be content and feel hyggely.

9. **Indulge without guilt**. Hygge doesn't do guilt, but it does do food. How to eat all the gorgeous things around and not have guilt? The answer is: don't. Not all the time, at least.

   Choose your treats, balance your meals and live well most of the time so that when you need a hygge treat you can indulge without guilt. The key word is balance: not too much, not too little.

10. **Build your soundtrack.**

Music has a massive effect on us. I am a complete sucker, and I only need a couple of notes of my trigger music to play and I can be bawling my head off. It really does affect our emotions. So think carefully about the soundtrack to your hygge and use a music service like Spotify to create the playlist for your hygge. Will it be gentle jazz, classical strings, soft rock or a real punk anarchy sound? I can't say, because you and you alone know the music that means something to you.

My soundtrack would have music right the way from the 1980s to now. No, scrub that. It would have some classical on as well. Oh, and classic Big Band sounds. Perhaps a little 1920's jazz. Eclectic, that's my genre.

11. **Write a letter to a person you are indebted to and post it**.

We did this once as part of a Bible study. I wrote to my Primary School head teacher, who was so beautifully down to earth that you would never have had her down for a nun! She always had time for people, was angry only for good reasons and could always see the funny side of events.

I found in writing to her that I had to clarify my own thoughts on why I owed her so much, and in doing that I saw ways I could help other people.

We are always copying behaviour: our choice is to copy good behaviour or bad. Learning to resist bad influences and to follow our own lights is one of the hardest things we do as human beings.

In writing my letter to Sister Tom, I had to sum up how I'd benefited. And it made me a better person, because I had my role model and I wanted to be like her. A smiling face to most people, but capable of righteous anger when necessary. Forgiving of human foibles and so well aware of her own. Always helping someone, but ready to stop and drink tea at the drop of a hat. I had a good role model.

12. Wanting to make life more cosy for the soul will never have an end.

There isn't a result to frame or a cup to display. It's an ever-changing thing, an on-going process. We never achieve nirvana, that blissful state of happiness.

That's why hygge works well, because it is so much more about the process than the result. We're not looking to be happy forever, we're looking to be happy for now. It pulls us into the present, it keeps us mindful.

And since there is no end destination, it makes sense to enjoy the ride. To enjoy the process of finding what makes you hyggely, because in finding that you will recognise yourself better. Although there may be common elements to most hygge, finding the particular sweet spot that suits you may take some searching, trying different stuff and being prepared to fail or to have a bad experience, to get up, shake yourself down and to move on to the next.

13. **Always have something to look forward to**.
Anticipation is gratitude for the future. In other words, the things you are looking forward to now are the things you will be grateful for later.

It's good to have plans and goals, but I'm talking about having some small events that you enjoy planned already, diaried up to take you through the wet Saturday, the too hot Wednesday afternoon, the meeting that the Boss made you sit through. Not even big events, just a coffee in your favourite café, a meeting planned with your friend on Saturday, a night at the cinema next week. Just a few forward planned hyggely moments to anticipate.

14. **I asked the Nookworms what they did to make their soul hyggelig**.
The most popular answer was to take time. Not to do or to read, to sew or to craft, but just to be.

In the end, we are Human Beings, not Doings. Perhaps ultimately what hygge calls us to do is to take that break from real life and just appreciate the good things we have.

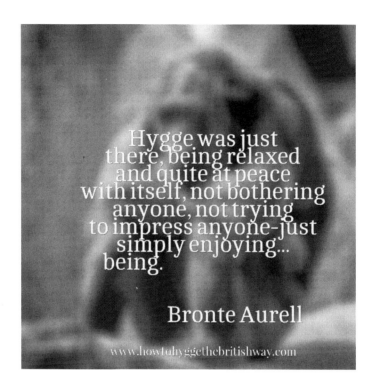

Hygge was just there, being relaxed and quite at peace with itself, not bothering anyone, not trying to impress anyone-just simply enjoying... being.

Bronte Aurell

www.howtohyggethebritishway.com

And there you have it. 50(ish) ideas to foster the experience of hygge in your life. It can't be caught and it won't be bought. You need to recognise it when you feel it, and I can't help you with that. Good luck on your hygge journey and do, please, get in touch if you've benefited from this book.

5: Hygge Resources

Hygge Books

I love me a good book, and I'll buy books ad infinitum on a subject I love. I think I bought nearly every book with Hygge in the title published in 2016 and 2017. Heck, I'll probably buy my own book as well, I'm that daft. I also reviewed many of them on the blog, How To Hygge The British Way.

It does mean, fortunately, that I can give you a flying resume on them all and tell you which I found most useful or not for my study of hygge. In no particular order, my recommendations are:

The Little Book of Hygge by Meik Wiking: I love this book especially as a starter reference for friends who have only the vaguest notion what hygge is. Meik exp;lains it simply and using examples from his own life. He also has the statistics to show why Denmark is the Happiest Place in the World. And the hygge manifesto he has compiled needs to be available as a poster. Really, it does.

The Essence of Hygge by Bronte Aurell: Bronte runs Scandinavian Kitchen in the heart of London, and has several cookbooks under her belt. The Essence of Hygge is basically Bronte's thoughts on hygge, but with added recipes. Her wisdom can teach us much about the importance of family in hygge, about appreciating the small things and about using food as the cement that holds a family together. I wish this book had been out last year when I was still learning about hygge.

Scandinavian Fika and Hygge by Bronte Aurell: Again with the Bronte!! This time a recipe book, and a very good one, with most Scandinavian treat recipes that you could want. It includes Loki's Brownies, because they look different every time you make them, and a fab recipe for Kladdkaka. I love kladdkaka.

Hygge: The Danish Art of Happiness by Marie Tourell Soderberg: Marie is an actress who lives in Copenhagen. She writes a beautiful book, full of beautiful people, and illustrated with beautiful photographs. What's lovely is she does know what she's talking about, and the writing is very down to earth, so you never feel like it's just an article from Hello! Or just another celebrity telling us how to live. I like that down to earth quality.

The Book of Hygge by Louisa Thomsen Brits: This one's the intellectual offering. Louisa's book is full of quotes and reference material, enough to make you wonder whether you couldn't do a PhD on hygge. You probably can, somewhere. Louisa's book isn't too dry for all that. She has combined the facts and history with a lighter writing touch. It's not for the absolute beginner, but for the person who has enjoyed learning how to hygge and now wants to know why.

The Cosy Life by Pia Edberg: One of the first books I read. Pia is Danish crossed with Phillippine living in America. She writes such a practical guide to living a cosy life, with advice on work,housing and fun. Her illustrations are line drawings but they're done by her, which must earn brownie points.

Scandinavian Comfort Food by Trinne Hahnemann: A collection of recipes that capture the Scandinavian food style. These are lovely old fashioned family recipes, but Trinne also has a diet book out that would encourage anybody to eat rye bread and herring for lunch.

And some to avoid: I really can't recommend these.

Hygge: A Danish Concept of Cosy and Simple Living by Noah Nielsen: Noah Nielsen must be into mindfulness as well, because this book is a mindfulness guide, right down to eating a grape mindfully. I couldn't recommend this to a beginner at exploring hygge, simply because I think it gives the wrong idea. Hygge isn't a new name for mindfulness. It isn't a retreat from the world. It's hygge. Lighten up!

Hygge by Charlotte Abrahams: I really wish I could recommend this, I do. But Charlotte looks at hygge as an Experiment to try in her life. The book sounds like it's been written by a woman who wanted to write a different book and got co-opted into writing this so that the publisher would have a Hygge book to put on the shelf in Autumn 2016 so they wouldn't be left out of the stampede. Charlotte really wanted to write about running. I really hope she gets the chance to, because her love of running comes through the book.

Hygge Blogs

What kind of blogger would I be if I didn't push a few blogs your way? Starting, of course, with mine.

https://howtohyggethebritishway.com/ is a look at how to get the important qualities of hygge (family, safety, appreciating time) to work in a 21st century British home. There are recipes, book reviews and plenty of opinion (mine). I also post links to my Facebook page.

https://hellohygge.com/ is by one of my favourite hygge bloggers, Kayleigh Tanner. She's like the opposite of me: young, single, working in London, living in Brighton, free to be… Her blog has books, opinion pieces and affiliate links.

http://hyggehouse.com/ is written by Alex Beauchamp. She's based in California, but her blog travels the world. It's full of lifestyle, hygge, books…

Of course, not every hyggely blog has hygge in the title. Here are just a few of my favourites:

http://attic24.typepad.com/ Lucy lives in Skipton and is a crazy crochet mother. Her blog, full of stories of everyday life, is like taking a quick break with a mate over coffee. She's lovely in real life as well, but oh so delicately small!

http://posy.typepad.com/ Posy (a Jane in real life) blogged until ill health made her stop. The archives are still available, though, and show wonderful real life just the way you want it to be.

http://rosylittlethings.typepad.com/ Posy Gets Cosy is the title of this American blog. She shares life, creativity and her story as an adoptive mother with beautiful (and I mean beautiful) photographs and a simple, friendly style.

https://cocorosetextiles.blogspot.co.uk/ A recommended read for me earlier this year, I traced the story of Ness' life back. Lovely, intimate writing. Again, plenty of really good pictures to accompany it.

Hygge Quotes

I use Quotescover.com on the internet to make my own hygge quotes. If you like any of them, get in touch and I'll send you the file. Otherwise, Pinterest is full of hygge quotes and inspirational quotes to help you create a loving and lovely life. Be warned: it does suck time away into a vortex.

Other Places to Find Hygge

Facebook has several groups dedicated to hygge. They're mostly closed groups, so you'll have to ask to join. My favourite, simply because I started it, is The Hygge Nook https://www.facebook.com/groups/TheHyggeNook/ which gives me my daily hygge-fix on days when I'm short on time or just desperate to talk to another hygge fan. There are off-shoot groups for books, crafts and recipes as well.

In real life: go out and join a group. A reading group, a painting group, a children's uniformed organisation. Anywhere where you will meet people who have something in common with you. And then work at the friendship. Building the bond to create hygge involves building a friendship based on trust, so be prepared to spend time working on it first. But once you have a group of friends that you can happily while away an evening with, go for it. Go and have some fun, and I wish you plenty of hygge at the same time.

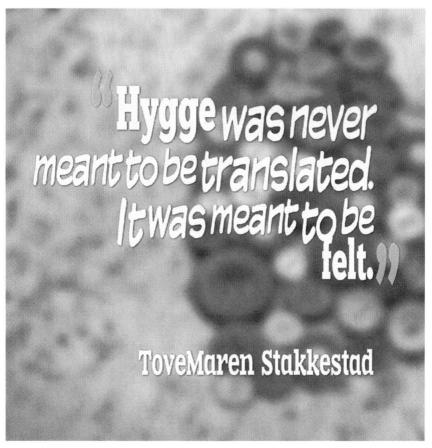

"Hygge was never meant to be translated. It was meant to be felt."

ToveMaren Stakkestad

A Word About Untranslatable Words:

No word is completely untranslatable. It's just that the time spent putting the concept into English takes too long and uses far more words than we're necessary. Far better and easier to nick the untranslatable and just use that. Once a concept has entered society and enough people are using it in a way close enough to the original, then the word won't need translating. It just is.

Printed in Great Britain
by Amazon